.

Grief and *Hope*—The Journey to Serenity

Dr Ann Ragobar

BALBOA.
PRESS
A DIVISION OF HAY HOUSE

Balboa Press books may be ordered through booksellers or by contacting:

Balboa Press
A Division of Hay House
1663 Liberty Drive
Bloomington, IN 47403
www.balboapress.com
1-(877) 407-4847

Because of the dynamic nature of the Internet, any web addresses or links contained in this book may have changed since publication and may no longer be valid. The views expressed in this work are solely those of the author and do not necessarily reflect the views of the publisher, and the publisher hereby disclaims any responsibility for them.

ISBN: 978-1-4525-5809-7 (sc)
ISBN: 978-1-4525-5810-3 (e)
ISBN: 978-1-4525-5811-0 (hc)

Library of Congress Control Number: 2012916576

The author of this book does not dispense medical advice or prescribe the use of any technique as a form of treatment for physical, emotional, or medical problems without the advice of a physician, either directly or indirectly. The intent of the author is only to offer information of a general nature to help you in your quest for emotional and spiritual well-being. In the event you use any of the information in this book for yourself, which is your constitutional right, the author and the publisher assume no responsibility for your actions.

Any people depicted in stock imagery provided by Thinkstock are models, and such images are being used for illustrative purposes only. Certain stock imagery © Thinkstock.

Printed in the United States of America

Balboa Press rev. date: 09/12/2012

This Book is dedicated to:

Wayne, my husband, love and best friend who taught me so much; but more importantly he taught me that we are never alone.

To the higher powers who are my Guides and Angels, thank you for your continued guidance through this storm of life and for helping me to recognize that we are never alone.

This is for the many people out there that have lost loved ones and for those that will lose loved ones in the future.

CONTENTS

ACKNOWLEDGEMENTS

A few years ago a very dear fellow walked into my life by the name of Casey Moran. He is a Psychic Medium and started working with me to bring to the surface the psychic gifts and talents that I have had well hidden since birth. Casey taught me the meaning of the word trust, he taught me to go within, remain in the silence and allow spirit to speak and guide me. He is one of a few that told me I would write books that would help many. To him I say "Thank you, dear friend for your encouragement and support."

The completion of this book would never have happened if it wasn't for (NC) who came into my life at a time, when I had no more energy to give. So, he lovingly gave me of his own energy, trust and support. All I can say is, "Thank you" from the depths of my soul.

To my Hawaiian Ohana (family), Mahalo Nui Loa for all your love, encouragement and support. Without all of you these pages would not be written.

My heart felt appreciation goes to my dear friend Sandra, who did the one last time look at this script. Sandra Shrieve and her family has been an inspiration, they have accepted me for who I am. For this I am eternally grateful.

Christine Francis of Ask Your Angels, she was very instrumental with the first edit as well as instrumental in confirming the book's title.

Carol-Ann Kirby who was not only a great help with the final edit but she is also a very gifted artist. Her painting is what graces this book cover.

Mary Ellen Brock who has been a dear friend for more years than I care to count has been not only a support system over the years. But is also a gifted photographer, even though at times she doubts her abilities.

At this time I would also like to acknowledge Wayne's sister Karen, who gave of her time and talent as an artist to create the black and white picture of her brother. She captures the very essence of the gentleman.

This list can go on, but to all of those that have impacted my life and my work in such positive ways. I will now extend my heartfelt thanks and deep appreciation.

FOREWORD

If I were going through a tremendous loss in my life, this would be the one book I would want to have available to me. I wish it had been here for me with past losses of loved ones, both two legged and four legged cherished beings.

Understanding some of the turbulent emotions we go through with a loss, and the whole roller-coaster of a ride to be faced is sometimes insurmountable. This book is a blessing and I thank you Dr. Ann.

In my work I deal with helping others through their physical discomforts. It has not been as comfortable for me to know how to help someone with their losses, and you have shed great insight into how to truly be able to help.

I will re-read, and re-read this book when necessary; when I need a reminder of how to cope as best I can with my own loved ones passing on, and when I need to be of service to others who will require friends/loved ones to see them through their grieving process.

As any journey goes, there is a beginning, and there is an ending, a moving on. The light you shed on how to best try to get through is a great gift to all and a help in understanding that there is always a new beginning for both the one who is grieving and the one who has passed.

I know first hand the comfort your presence brings when dealing in this matter, and I cherish the gift you have as well as this gift you have given.

Sandra Shrieve
Certified Biofeedback Specialist
Quantum Synergy Co.

PREFACE

My life has always been filled with extraordinary events. However, the most challenging and the one which would bring me to my knees was my partner, Wayne's illness. In November 2008 he contracted what we thought was a simple case of pneumonia. This one initial event would put us both on first a medical path and then a life altering journey neither of us wanted nor were prepared to deal with.

We had lived full and productive lives; loving each other with every fibre of our being. We did most things, including the mundane of everyday life, together. Having both been in relationships before we recognized that this relationship was special – perhaps being divinely guided.

Wayne had intuitive knowledge but it was not something that he focused his attention on. However, as time went by, he was learning to become more aware and trusting of this intuitive knowledge or gut instinct. He believed in the Divine and was aware that he was truly never alone; he and we are being divinely guided.

Our journey culminated with Wayne's death from cancer and my life's journey without him was to begin. It had never dawned on me that I would have to learn to live again, Live without his physical presence, without his nurturing love and support. Frightened and lonely I would begin my new journey alone; making my own mistakes and learning valuable lessons along the way.

This book is based on my own experiences; my life lessons learned and are still learning since Wayne's passing. As a Final Phase Transitional Facilitator (in private practice helping families and their loved ones deal with end of life issues). My sincere hope and prayer is that the words conveyed within these pages will help to soothe some of the fears and concerns that families have when the end of life issues arise.

I have chosen to honour not only Wayne and his memory but all of our loved ones who have gone before us. Life is a journey that is meant to be shared.

Namaste

Ann

Leo Buscaglia author of the book "Love"
describes the word " Namaste"
I honor the place in you where the entire universe resides.
I honor the place in you, where lies your love,
your light, your truth and your beauty.

I honor the place in you, where ......if you are in that place in
you....and I am in that place in me.....then There is only one of us.
Namaste
is often used as a form of greeting.

INTRODUCTION

After Wayne's diagnosis and subsequent passing I was left with a void in my life and I needed to find out how to cope with this pain and loneliness. I bought books, many too lengthy for a grief stricken attention span. So through trial and error I tried to listen to words on pages and to my own instincts.

The objective in writing this little book is to help make your journey easier.

As a spiritual person and an intuitive I will share with you the tools you need to get you through this difficult time. You will learn to trust your "gut instinct". Trust in prayer, meditation and other holistic methods which allow us to fine tune our own intuitive knowing which connects us with the Divine (whoever that may be in your world).

Death is not an ending but rather a new journey for our loved ones crossing over. You will see, hear and speak to your loved ones again and what a glorious reunion that will be.

The journey to serenity after the loss of a loved one is not easy, but it is attainable given time.

All of us share an intuitive knowing; otherwise referred to as our "gut instinct". Prayer, meditation, and other holistic methods allow us to fine tune our intuitive knowing connecting us with a Divine, authentic authority. Through faith, desire and trust, hope is attainable!!

As a spiritual intuitive, I will share my talents by explaining what I know. Death is not an ending. There is survival after death; a new journey for our loved ones crossing over. You will see, hear and speak to your loved ones again!! What a glorious reunion that will be!!

Despite being spirit beings, our earthly existence exposes us to pain; especially that of a great loss. We can transition; from grief to hope, and ultimately our Journey to Serenity.

Dr. Ann Ragobar

DIVINE

– means

The spiritual aspect in humans regarded as Godly or Godlike.

Coping With Grief

Coping With Grief

Some times in life, situations can arise that can literally bring us to our knees; such as the death of a loved one.

Here is my story:

Grief is a journey that we must take at some point in our lives. The million dollar question is: How do we cope with grief?

In January, Wayne, my soul mate, husband and best friend was diagnosed with cancer. The universe gave us the privilege (trust me, I do call it a privilege)

of two and a half months of remaining time together. We spent hours talking, laughing and naturally, crying. We knew that the end was near. He did not want to die at home; knowing the memory of this passing would be a constant reminder as long as I resided in our home.

Though I respected his decision, I tried to encourage him to pass his last few weeks at home but Wayne stood firm.

Wayne's decision not to be resuscitated (DNR) was difficult for me emotionally but intellectually I agreed with his decision. Though heart wrenching for me, we did not want to prolong his agony and pain any longer than necessary.

Much time was spent at the hospital. His sister, niece and I took shifts at the hospital to ensure he had company at all times. It also gave us the opportunity to ask appropriate questions of the medical staff.

Each person visiting Wayne experienced a great deal of healing and forgiveness. He was an encouragement to others, despite his own pain. Many of his colleagues came to spend time with him; reminiscing about work and the old days.

My visits with Wayne, mainly spent talking, were very precious to me. Constantly he reminded me that I had an abundance of divine help. Wayne tried giving me hope. In my heart I knew that he was right; yet I knew what was coming. Late at night, returning home, I would, break down and cry. I felt so alone.

One day I asked Wayne, though only fifty seven, if he accomplished everything in his life he wanted to do. His reply was, "Yes. The biggest worry I have is leaving you, for I know how difficult you will find my passing."

On March 22, his niece and I spent the night with Wayne in the Palliative Care Unit. In and out of consciousness for a good portion of the night Wayne and I knew that the end was near. He kept saying to me, that "this world is not my home, I was just passing through". We also knew that he was fighting to stay alive for "us". Probably the most difficult thing that any one will do in their life time is what his niece and I did next. Verbally giving him permission to go to our *Eternal Home*, we offered reassurance. Even though we would miss him dearly, it was time for him to rest.

At 7:48 am, on March 23, 2009 I saw Wayne take his final three breaths of life. Twenty minutes passed, though time seems to stand still. Finally I said, "*So long to him for now; till we meet again*". In life, whenever, I am really stressed or could not sleep, Wayne would gently rub the back of my head, to help me relax. In those twenty minutes following his departure, I felt Wayne's hand tenderly rubbing the back of my head.

In meditation, three weeks before Wayne passed; a white envelope was shown to me. I was told the envelope contained Wayne's next assignment on the other side. Prepared to leave this earth, he so eloquently said "*Ann this world is not my home. My only regret is leaving you*" Leave me he did, I thought that I was prepared for his passing...... NOT!! Even though he is physically not with me, I firmly believe that he is guiding me from the other side. We have the most interesting conversations." Here is an example of such a conversation:

On one exceptionally cold Easter Sunday morning I was putting fresh flowers on Wayne's grave. I heard him asking me how crazy I was putting flowers on what is now his shell. Did I not realize he is still with me in spirit? Yes, I know he is with me in spirit, but I loved the shell also that carried his soul and spirit. This was part of him. Wayne remained quiet for just a few minutes, only to say, *"Ann, you are shivering with the cold temperatures.* Get back in the warmth of the vehicle." Although on another plane, Wayne was still taking care of me. Trust me I did what I was told.

Shortly after this experience at the cemetery while I was in meditation one morning I heard several of my guides admonishing me not to take my vehicle on the road. I was grieving the loss of Wayne so I did not pay attention.

While I was out that morning, driving along one of our busiest highways a light flashed on the dashboard of the vehicle.

The following morning, again in meditation I was told "Do not move the vehicle off the driveway. As a matter of fact, stop your meditation, get the keys, and head outside and check the oil; Ann, check the oil."

I proceeded outside, opened up the hood. Good start, now what? Checking the oil, how does one do this? Well I remembered watching Wayne check the vehicles, but right now I could not put two sane thoughts together. So, between Wayne and my guides, here is the conversation that we had:

Wayne: Ann, look for the dipstick, the long stick that looks like it has an "O" on it. You will see this towards the front of the engine and it will say oil." Ok, I found it!!! I remembered how he used to check to see if there was oil or not. So I did, guess what? There was not one drop of oil in the reservoir. Oh joy! So how does one fill up the oil without getting it all over the engine? Oh, my guides please help!! My next thought was to take the vehicle to the mechanic.

My guides all in unison screamed, NOOOO you cannot move the vehicle!!!! You can do what the mechanic would do. We are here."

Wayne: Ann, go into the garage you will see oil." Off I go. Ok, but there is umpteen containers of the stuff. Which one? Panic set in!!

"Relax Ann, it's the green container." Found that, now, how does one pour the stuff into the engine with getting it all over the engine?

Wayne: Ann dear, please quiet your mind for a minute. I made a funnel to use for pouring oil into the engine, please take a look around. It should be where the oil is." Nope, I cannot find it. One of my guides asked me to check on one of the shelves which are to the left of where I was standing. And there it is the funnel! Oh, thank god for small mercies.

With that, and with very steady hands (trust me it was the angels holding my hands, I was such a nervous wreck) I used two containers of oil that morning. In a conversation a few weeks later our mechanic told me that no oil in the engine could have killed the vehicle completely.

So we cope by remembering, *we are never alone* (even though at times we feel that we are). Our Angels, Guides and our loved ones are around us. Slowly; very gently we pick ourselves up, and dust ourselves off; we put one foot in front of the other; and take each day one minute at a time.

Make goals for yourself. Work towards them. Spend time out-doors; walk, meditate, garden, paint. Do whatever makes your heart a little lighter. Reach out to help someone else! But more importantly, honour your own feelings.

Remember that we have all been blessed with unique gifts and talents. Find out what they are and use them. (Wayne always encouraged me to use my talents to help others and I am now doing so)

Loneliness is getting to me, I do not have siblings. Wayne and I did not have children. Yet as I mentioned earlier, our loved ones are all around.

Remember the things that your loved ones taught you, remember what made them unique. I quoted in giving Wayne's eulogy, Francois Mauriac …. *"We are, all of us moulded by those who have loved us. And even though the love may pass, we remain never the less.. "Their Work". It is a work they very likely do not recognize and it is not exactly what they intended. No Love and No Friendship can EVER cross the path of our DESTINY without leaving some mark upon it FOREVER."*

Please remember, grief takes time. It begins by taking things minute by minute; hour by hour and eventually day by day. It is a journey, walk that road with *courage, trust, grace* and *dignity*. Know that our loved ones along with our angels are walking besides us, even holding us up as is needed. In time all will be well!!!

As for me I walk this road minute by minute, reaching out; helping others whose loved ones have been diagnosed with a terminal illness.

Never Alone

At times we feel the loneliness
At times we feel sad
At times we think that no one cares

We are never alone
At night when darkness surrounds us
At night when sleep is thus denied

We are never alone

Our ever present friends are our angels and our guides
They quell our fears
They soothe our restless soul
Their presence can be felt in various ways

We are never alone
Our angels and our guides walk with us each
and every day
They help us in every way
They guide our thoughts
They guide our steps
They teach us life lessons
They try to keep us safe from harm
We are never alone
So when darkness falls and the night surrounds
us
Our angels and our guides will abide with us if only for a while
They will even sing us a lullaby if we would only
ask

May we always remember that we are never alone
May we always be thankful to our angels and our
guides

For they make sure that we do not face life and its
challenges alone

NOTES

On Death and Dying

The thought of Death and the subsequent result of *Dying* are two of the most feared and misunderstood words in our language. This is true the world over. Death can be described as a journey or transition that takes place for each and every one of us; you cannot run or hide from death or the effects it has on us and our loved ones.

For years, many religions instilled a sense of foreboding when we die, any sins committed in this life, will be settled in the afterlife. Some teach that we will sleep for thousands of years, awakening to a resurrection or damnation. Anyone experiencing these teachings, naturally, would be terrified to die.

When someone has been told they will die from a diagnosed illness, fear grips their mind and heart. The reality of death is not to be feared by any of us. As a matter of fact, embrace it as your soul's natural journey; a necessary evolution to *Divine*. Permit me to shine a little light on this journey and transition of our soul.

Through meditations and conversations with several on the other side, including my guides, I have been told that the process one goes through at death is fairly simple. It was explained this way: Just as you go to bed at night; you fall asleep with all the pains and health issues associated with your physical body. Opening your eyes on the other side, you will see a bright white light, welcoming you home. Some of your loved ones along with your guides will await your return. No longer carrying the burdens of a sick and tired body; aches and pains diminish no more medical treatments to endure. If at one time you could not walk, now you will run!!! If your lungs were diseased and you could not breathe now great gulps of fresh, pure air fill every inch of your body. Having suffered from failing eyesight or perhaps being blind you will be able to appreciate the vast array of colors. You will look in awe at the luscious green meadows. And truly begin to appreciate all that you once could not see.

Upon arrival on the other side a loving welcome awaits you!! Your earthly journey now complete, expect rewards of hugs, kisses, and unconditional love! It's a true welcome home. A time for rest and rejuvenation, particularly if there was a major illness involved. You will find peace and pure joy enveloping you.

A *Council of Elders* along with your guides await your *Life Review;* a loving evaluation of what paths you traveled while on earth. It is not a judgement! All the while, Divine's unconditional love fills your spirit.

You may ask." *How do you know these things? Is this true? Have you seen this?"*

Through a *Past Life Regression* and a procedure called *Life In Between Lives* (a session involving *Hypnotherapy*) I, like many others, have *seen the other side.* Shot and killed in my most recent past life, the scene unfolded as I hovered and looked over my lifeless body, the person that took my life and the crowd that had gathered around me.

Turning my head I saw a bright white light with a royal blue tinge. I knew it was time to journey home. Walking through the light for me was akin to walking on a beautiful beach at three in the morning. Feeling a gentle breeze on my face, I basked in the warmth of pure love, calmness, and peace. Intertwined with voices of loved ones, were the gentle, rolling sounds of the ocean waves; once again, welcoming me home.

I have also had the privilege of speaking to a few people that have had near death experiences. They were very helpful in validating what I have seen through meditation

Everyone's experience is unique to them. Yet the light is always there, guiding us; as is the eternal unconditional love of the Divine.

Thus death is not to be feared or misunderstood; it is not the end of all things. Death is nothing more than a small part of the journey we all must travel; a starting point to the soul's next step toward the Divine. The physical body decays; the soul is eternal; returning home to be with loved ones and the Divine Creator. Embrace the journey!! There is no Hell in which to spend everlasting damnation.

As for those who have just lost loved ones or for those who have loved ones at the end stage of life it is a grief stricken time. Try to remember the separation is temporary. Those in pain on earth, close their eyes; awakening to renewed health and unconditional love. As our loved ones cross over their love for us does not die, it is limitless and ever increasing.

NOTES

Diagnosis

As a family member, you probably knew for many months something was terribly wrong with your loved one. There were probably numerous doctors visits, endless medical tests and many nights of worry and the thought patterns of "what if". Instinctively as a family you knew that the tests results would not be good.

The medical lab reports have come back and a subsequent discussion with the medical specialist indicates that the illness is terminal!

As a family member helping a friend or a loved one, yes you knew something was wrong, but this news is shocking, almost mind blowing.

In respect to Wayne's illness we both knew what was coming before the doctor's diagnosis. It does not matter how much a person knows, the news is still a shock.

As a family, each person handles the news differently; in their own way. If your family is accustomed to openly communicating their feelings, it may be a tad easier discussing the illness and all of the what if's that come with it.

For very introverted families each one retreat to their own little world to absorb the information, emotions and feelings remain bottled up. Thus, they manifest their own physical and emotional symptoms, causing more concern to family and friends.

Household Changes

With a terminal diagnosis, normalcy within the family ceases to exist. Daily hospital visits are the new normality. Suddenly one partner is ill while the other juggles work and home along with new found and unfamiliar emotions

The healthy partner wants to spend as much time as they can with the ailing loved one. Perhaps he can get a leave of absence from his job – (this would depend on the company and its policies)

Get Outside Help

All information given applies to any family member, spouse or friend that is a support system for someone that has a terminal illness. The term "Dad" is used for simplification purposes.

1. Consider family counselling. Raw nerves; stressed-out dad, children clinging to the only parent available at home. It is no wonder a spouse of ordinarily good nature is somewhat ill-mannered. Tempers are bound to flare. Sometimes all you want to do is cry. Do it. Crying can be very cathartic
2. For the interim, find someone to clean and grocery shop.
3. If your loved one is at home hire a home care nurse. Although humanly possible, do not attempt to take responsibility for all the *full* care of your loved one. It might be humanly possible but NOT humanly **responsible** to take on this duty alone. You will burn-out.

(If the patient has cancer, have someone look into what provisions the Cancer Society makes for helping the patients. In some cases they provide transportation to and from hospital visits. Consult with them!!!)

(Also have someone look into what the local CCAC (Community Care Access Centre) can provide. Delegating this research to someone else is okay as people want to help.

4. If nothing more can be done once all medical avenues are explored, then access your community hospice care. Unfortunately death is something that cannot be denied. People who work in hospices are experts who help the terminally ill to die with dignity.

Families leave this step as the very last resort – By looking into hospice care the family has to acknowledge the probability of the inevitable passing. This is not easy.

Funeral Planning

5. This is the most difficult task to face. Whether pre-planning or coming to terms with the inevitable passing or perhaps your loved one has crossed over, you are now faced with the reality of making final arrangements.

My husband was very hands- on with planning his own funeral. Although in much pain, he did not want me to have to face this stage alone. We went to the funeral home together to speak with the funeral director. Wayne voiced his wishes. Trust me this was absolutely heartbreaking for me.

As a matter of fact, shortly before he passed; I was on my way to work, Wayne called me and requested that I purchase a plot for him that has a tree near the driveway in the cemetery. So I asked him why he wanted a tree, his reply was "Dear I want you to purchase a bench that will be placed under the tree. This way when you come to see me, you will not have to walk far and you can have a place to sit." Yes, I did as he requested!!

After Wayne passed, I was so thankful we had pre-planned; making things a bit easier. Usually after someone passes away, there is so much to do, and so many things to remember. In our case, I made the decision to give Wayne's eulogy; it was my final tribute to him.

Regrets and Forgiveness

6. In some cases, when a loved one passes on, the remaining family (and sometimes friends) go through a period of regret. It could be as *simple* as regret over not having communicated with the deceased on a regular basis *before* he passed or it could be as *complicated* as a rift that caused a parting of the ways. That rift was never mended. No communication. No visits. *Now* it is too late.

If there is a rift between you and another person mend fences, extend to them the olive branch of kindness. Reach out. Try to communicate with them. If they do not reciprocate your kindness do not take this personally. But know that you would have nothing to regret, if you ever heard of their passing. At least you tried!! But at the same time, *forgive* whatever *they* may or may not have done.

The bible advises "*Do not go to bed angry*". In truth, we never know what tomorrow may or may not bring. Remember, words *spoken*, things *done*, remain in the past. It cannot be *un*done. But you can certainly learn from it; forgive it and move forward.

Spirituality

7. What is *spirituality*? Many would ask ---*How does spirituality relate to grieving?*

First of all, spirituality is not morality (morality can be defined as an instilled set of social mores, a measuring stick for what is good in the society).

Spirituality can be defined as things above human limitations such as faith, hope, loyalty and love. In a physical world our soul reveals many things about our spiritual values. Spirituality deals with the "why" of life. It makes us ask/ question the most fundamental things in life. Such as: *Why do we die? What happens to us when we cross over? Is there judgment, the way that religion teaches us?*

I am blessed with the monumental help of many angels and guides and the ability to be able to answer some of these questions. Much of this guidance is given through my work.

Sometimes fears that the patient might have can begin with the housekeeping questions, such as, *what happens to my home after I am gone? Later the questions become more about what happens after I leave this earth* and transition to the other side. They may be terrified to die and afraid to see what awaits them. The poem entitled "Afraid to Die" is words and anxieties that can come from a patient. I created this piece of poetry to help you the reader get a better sense of some of the fears.

Afraid To Die

My days are numbered
This I know for sure
The pain within my body is teeth grinding
There is no medication that can relieve the pain within my heart

Afraid to Die

My days are spent in deep reflection
I think upon the life that I have lived
I think up on the afterlife of which I know nothing

Afraid to Die

I was taught there is a hell
I was taught there is nothing beyond this life
I was taught that god punishes badness
Before I take my last breath can someone please
tell me about the other side

I am so afraid to die
I reflect on my family
What happens to my house
What happens to my car
We worked hard for what we have
I did not plan with death in mind
I did not make a will

Afraid to Die
My eyes will close for the last time
I worry about that family of mine
I was always their rock
I was always their strength
Who will see them through this sad time
Can someone please spare me some time
I am afraid to die

NOTES

Most of all they seek some form of inner peace. Some might do a *life review*; by writing their memoirs; documenting their life story. Others will speak of their accomplishments or feel sorrow for not accomplishing certain things in their life.

Remember to always be a good listener when a person is doing their life review. Do not judge, do not analyze or importantly, *do not criticize*. Also do not trivialize the speaker's words. It is very important that the patient is able to express their fears, anger and doubts to someone who accepts them completely. This is their journey, not yours!!!!!!!

Listen With Your Heart

Author Unknown
One author expressed it this way:

When I ask you to listen to me and your start giving advice
You have not done what I have asked….

When I ask you to listen to me and you being to tell me why
I shouldn't feel that way; you are trampling on my feelings

When I asked you to listen to me and you feel you have to do
something to solve my problems, you have failed me, strange
as that may seem

Listen!!!!

All I asked was that you listen, not talk or do ----Just hear me

Advice is cheap!!

A quarter will get you both Dear Abby and Billy Graham in the
same newspaper. And I can do for myself

I am not helpless!!

When you do something for me that I can and need to do for myself,
you contribute to my fear and inadequacy

But when you accept as a simple fact that
I do feel what I feel, no matter
how irrational then I can quit trying to convince you and can get the
business of understanding what is this irrational feeling
And when that's clear, the answers are
obvious and I don't need advice"

Always listen with an open heart and mind
to those whose life has been
turned down and inside out by the passing of a loved one!!!

Just listen!!!

Author Unknown.

NOTES

Caregiver Burnout

People do not burnout because they are busy, the burnout because they neglect themselves (sound familiar)

Burnout: Occurs over time and leads to a state of mental, emotional and physical exhaustion.

Physical Symptoms of Burnout:
-Fatigue
-Sleep Disruption
-Body Aches and Pains
-Headaches
-Low Immune System
-Absenteeism – decline in productivity

Emotional and Behavioural Systems
-Anxiety
-Depression
-Helplessness
-Isolation
-Carelessness
-Irritability
-Substance Abuse

Care For Burnout

- Be gentle with yourself. Think of it this way, if you burn yourself out you have nothing in reserve for your loved ones.

- Enlist the help of others to be at the hospital when you cannot be there.

- You have a life. You probably have a family. Your role as *Caregiver* should not negate these.

- You might have secular employment. Your employers might be kind hearted people who emphasize with your situation. However, they will only give you so much leeway. Try to work, even if it is part-time as this may help you to stay focused.

- Pray & Meditate

- Find your "*happy place*"; a setting that is tranquil: perhaps a garden with soothing sounds from a nearby waterfall.

- Treat yourself to a spa day…..manicure….pedicure….. long soak in tub, whatever it takes to make you feel a bit *special*

- Vent when you have too

- Find a few minutes each day to be *"in the moment"*–Just breath; listening to the beat of your own heart.

- Journaling can also be very therapeutic…it transposes from your head on to the paper

- Music can also be soothing and therapeutic

Stress takes a very heavy toll on family and friends, when they are being supportive to a friend our family member that is ill. Here are some of the for instances as well as why stress could be apparent.

Stress in Palliative Care

Caregivers can have difficulty accepting that their loved ones pain cannot always be controlled.

Frustration when dealing with other member's of the family in addition to the patient.

Irritated with the amount of time and energy care can actually take.

You feel guilt-ridden that you actually feel exasperated by the situation.

Angry and frustrated at the medical personnel, who do not seem to pay much attention to your loved ones or worse yet they seem to ignore your questions.

At times you feel guilty for running out of patience as well as energy.

Angry, frustrated and tired at the amount of nights you seem obligated to spend at the hospital (Remember, in order to function, you need a good night's sleep.)

Feeling annoyed. This could entail anger towards the patient for getting sick, irritation at the medical professionals for what is deemed as not giving adequate care to the patient.

You may experience some anger at the patient for not fighting harder; or wanting to recover; particularly if they make the decision that they do not want to be resuscitated (DNR). I was recently attended at the bedside of a patient that stated she did not want to be resuscitated. The granddaughter was very angry at her grandmother. Yet after seeing the way the grandmother deteriorated the granddaughter did understand why resuscitating would almost be a criminal act. Bringing a loved one back to no quality of life after watching them deteriorate only prolongs the suffering; not only for the one that is ill but also for the family.

Here is a big one, angry at God! Try to remember, that he did not cause your loved ones illness, life happens.

Care For The Caregiver

A prognosis of the eventual passing of a loved one with advanced stages of illness can blindside family members and caregivers alike

Here are a few things that can take its toll on family members:

- The emotional rollercoaster ride from denial to acceptance of the *diagnosis* and *prognosis.*

- Getting to know the health care professionals who are caring for your loved one.

- Helping other family members to cope

- Family caregivers having secular employment

- The care and responsibility of a caregiver's own family.

- Meeting the needs of their ill loved one

- Discussing and trying to make decisions for the one that is ill.

In some cases allowing the patient to make their own choices while they are still able to do so.

Notice how this one comes last---***Taking Care of Yourself***

If you are a friend to a care giver, one of the best things you can do is to lend them your ear, listen to them. They need to speak, by doing this they can download some of the stress.

The Importance Of Journaling

Journaling is a process that can be very liberating. Once you start it can develop into a way of life that requires very little preparation.

All you need is a quiet space, a pen, notepad or computer. Don't worry about the grammar or sentence structure. There is no format to this. There is no right or wrong way to write. The idea is to take all the thoughts, events, worries and images out of your head and commit them to paper.

Remember keeping a diary when you were younger? After writing your thoughts down, you stashed it, in a secret place. Still, parents had a way of finding them; becoming privy to the information. And to tell you the truth this is what stopped me from writing.

However, over the past two years, journaling has become a mainstay in my life. I went back to journaling, when Wayne became ill. I would wake up in the middle of the night terrified of the what ifs. *What if the treatment does not work?? What if funds will not allow me to keep him at home? What if he dies?*

Committing all of these questions and fears to paper, although the questions did not go away, it helped me to place them in perspective. Putting down questions that are on one's mind, it actually helps to ease some of the fears.

Illness is a fear within itself. Committing some of the symptoms and feelings to paper can help the participant and healthcare provider decide which form of care to take.

My notebook has become my good friend. When I travel, my notebook comes with me. All of my fears, doubts, concerns (whether it is health related or not) are recorded on those pages. However, along with these, I also record desired intentions and outcomes.

So, what desired outcome would you like to see? With your given situation, recording positive intentions and outcomes on any situation will help imprint them on your subconscious mind. Our subconscious mind is where much of our fear is stored. It is amazing; when we review these pages, we can see how things have transpired.

I tell myself, "By putting things on paper, (particularly before going to sleep at night), releases them from my mind and body; allowing me to relax. The issues, now on paper, are not in my head.

Journaling can be very cathartic, particularly if you can envision the process of writing your stressful moments flowing from you on to the paper. In my experience, journaling can be very therapeutic for those doing the writing

Many people keep their journals by their bedside. By journaling before going to sleep it helps them organize their thoughts. Sometimes it also provides a solution to a problem.

When you start to journal, do not sit, trying to determine what is important to write. Do not do this. Write the first thing that comes to mind; whether it makes sense or not. The idea here is to take all the thoughts and ideas out of your head and place them onto paper.

Some people, like me, journal everyday. Others prefer doing this two or three times a week. Do whatever works and is comfortable for you.

When the reality of the illness sinks into the heart and mind of our a loved one, some times they might want to talk. Perhaps they would like to discuss their illness, diagnosis and in some instances worry sets into their heart and mind concerning other family members and how these ones are coping with the news.

As the caregiver or support system for someone that is ill we need to listen.

Here are a few tips that will help you to be a good listener.

NOTES

Listen With Love

1. ***SILENCE***—*is golden*. Definition; *STOP TALKING---* Listening is *learning*. Why are you talking?

2. **LOOK AT THEM**. Make eye contact. It is said, "*The eyes* are the *windows to the soul* ." Look at the eyes. They speak volumes that not even words can express.

3. **ENCOURAGEMENT** –Show interest in all the person is sharing with you. You can say such things as *"Tell me more", I would love to learn about such and such"*.

4. **CONCENTRATE ON WHAT IS BEING SAID**. Focus on the word\

5. Focus on the feelings.

6. **DO NOT INTERRUPT** –Allow them to speak. You can, however, encourage the conversation with short phrases such as, *"I see. Really? Then what?*

7. **REMEMBER THIS CONVERSATION IS NOT ABOUT YOU!!**

8. Set your emotions and judgments aside.

9. **RESPOND APPROPRIATELY** – smile, nod

10. **LEADING QUESTIONS** – Talk to me, what are you feeling? Tell me about your loved one? Let me help you, give me a grocery list, I will do the grocery shopping. These can help draw the person out allowing them to clarify their thoughts and feelings.

11. **ELIMINATE DISTRACTIONS** –Turn off the electronic devices, leave the pen on the table.
Playing with these distractions sends the message that:
(A) You do not care about the person speaking
(B)   You prefer to be someplace else Please develop the qualities of being a good listener!!

NOTES

Emotional Loss

Keys To Emotional Loss

As the caregiver of a sick family member, for many months you have been on a physical and emotional rollercoaster. Now they have passed, what do you do?

Burial preparations, along with greeting the friends and family members who have come to pay their respects, make the first few days quite hectic. As much as possible, pre-arrange the funeral. Usually, in the first few hours and days after a passing, the mind and body are completely numb. The more you pre-arrange, the easier it will be.

The funeral is over. Friends and relatives have gone back to their own lives. You are now left to handle your own grief, plus that of family members looking to you for support.

The **Four Stages of Grief** makes up the frame work of *learning to cope* with *loss*. Everyone grieves differently some of these listed might resonate with you, while other stages might not.

Denial

Denial kicks in when not even your own psyche will accept that fact that your loved one is gone. No more phone calls during the day. No more having them walk through the front door at the end of the day. Denial helps us to cope with the initial stages of shock. You might walk into a grocery store and see people *shopping, laughing, talking*, but for you the one *grieving*, the world has become meaningless; and in some cases overwhelming.

Coping

At this stage of denial, you will start to have questions such as: *How did this happen? Why did this happen? Did this have to happen? Is there anything I could have done to change the outcome?* You will also find yourself reviewing the circumstances of the loss. There is nothing wrong in doing this. As a matter of fact this is the first stage to begin the healing process.

Anger

Anger, has no limits, this emotion kicks in when, you realize that you *will* survive this tragedy. You might get angry at your loved one dying; angry that you are left behind to cope and move on with life. You might be angry with the doctors. You might be angry that you feel you did not look after your loved one properly. You might be angry at the fact that you did not anticipate this coming.

Your pain is coming out by way of anger. It's natural to feel alone, deserted. Well meaning friends might try to tell you that it is not right to be angry; that it is *misplaced* or even inappropriate. (Heaven help them the day they lose someone)

Vent

Honour your feelings. Honour the *anger*. Cry, jump, and scream from the highest spot you can find. Let it out!!! Vent these feelings whenever you have to, need to, this is a natural part of loss. Vent to a trusted friend or a counsellor. Do not try to analyze the feelings. You cannot change the past.

Anger lets you know that you have *lost big time*, yet you still feel, and more importantly, you still love. This feeling of anger will subside; trust me on this!

Depression

Depression causes sleep deprivation, lack of appetite, and lack of motivation. You feel heavy in body, mind and spirit. This is natural. (Personally I went through all of this; I lost 25lbs and to tell you the truth I did not have this weight to lose to begin with.) For me, the loss of Wayne, and subsequent stages of grief (such as depression) helped me to take a good, hard, long look at my life. It helped me to get my feet on a firm foundation. The loss helped me to take a look deep into my soul; finding out what my life's purpose is; where to go from here. How many of us really take time to take stock of our lives?

Acceptance

Acceptance; sums up as "believing". Believing this permanent reality; your loved one has passed. We learn to accept it as well as to live with it. Life is a journey. Though our journey was stopped temporarily with the passing of our loved one; we must pick up the pieces of our lives and move forward. Reflect on all the things that your loved one taught you or said to you. Many times the things that they said, are the very things that will help you to continue to heal and to live.

Whether you believe it or not, your life; is forever changed, because of this loss. As we heal we learn about ourselves and who our loved one was in life; we now draw on the many things they taught us. Acceptance means you will have good days and bad ones. Over time, you will open yourself up to others; you will make new connections form new bonds.

Grieving is a process. It takes *time*, it takes *patience* and more importantly it takes *courage*. But we all need to go through this process before we can fully integrate ourselves back into living our life.

Here is the key:

Find time to grieve. Many people jump right back into work and life, bury their grief so deep; only to discover years later, they still have not processed their emotions associated with their loss. Often it resurfaces later, with disastrous results. Please don't do this. ***Take the time! Grieve now!***

1. Seek out someone who has experienced the bereavement process first hand. They can help you walk this road; by giving you some clarity on how to do it.

2. Do what you enjoy, such as listening to music, gardening or perhaps meditation, do so! This will help. Joyous things help heal the heart.

3. Speak of your loved one as often as you choose. There are many things that you will have learned from them. And in the weeks and months to come, there will be lots of time to reflect on these things.

Often the person that has crossed held great significance in your life. Perhaps it was a father figure, who taught you to change a car tire, or even how to fix electrical wiring without killing yourself. Remember the joy of times spent together learning and doing such things. Remember the funny stories, the jokes they might have told you. Remember the much larger hand; that held yours the first time you tried to nail a two by two together; and instead of hitting the nail on the head; you hit your finger.

Perhaps it was Mom that has crossed over. Remember walking in her front door to the smell of home made bread. Oh, yummy!! Or perhaps it's the memories of her hugging you the first time your heart was broken! Remember the advice she gave you!!

As you see, they have not really left you. Physically yes; emotionally they are still with you guiding and admonishing. You just need to stand still long enough to listen to the messages.

Our loved ones taught us many things and in some cases made us who we are today. You will miss their physical presence; rightly so.

Throughout the grief process you must take the time to grieve. By doing so, we honour our feelings and our emotions. This process takes time. Be patient with yourself and others. Always honour the memories of your loved ones.

By speaking with someone who has suffered a loss and has been through the process will help you find some peace. They might be the only person to answer questions that no one else can.

If all else fails, please remember that despite the fact that the physical body is gone, the love they have for you did not die with them. If anything, it is stronger. The world they now inhabit is *pure love* and *peace*. Even though they are not with you in the physical body, they are always with you in spirit. When your soul leaves this earthly plane, you will have the privilege to meet and greet all those that have gone before you. In the meantime, honour your grief and those of your loved ones. This gives you the strength to help other family members cope. Death is another part of the "*journey of our soul.*" Life does go on in another plane of existence.

Child/Teen Grief

Child/Teen Grief

Grief for an adult can be difficult, but for a child/teenager it is harder yet. When the person who has passed is one of the child's guardians, this could be parents, grandparents; the child, at any age will be affected by the loss on a much larger scale.

Why is this?

1. Some are of the opinion that the child believes it is somehow their fault that the person passed.

Children particularly view the death as punishment for misbehaviour, or perhaps because they didn't show the parent enough love.

2. They go into *denial* mode. They child denies the reality of the passing; making the healing process much more difficult.

3. Some teens can become suicidal and have gone as far as committing suicide. I knew of a family where the grandmother resided with her daughter and grandchildren. The children shared a very close relationship with the grandmother who subsequently

passed. Three weeks after the passing of the grandmother one of the granddaughters took her own life. She could not cope with the grandmother's absence.

4. When there is a death in the family it is vital that child/teenager get some kind of counselling or at least a listening ear.

5. A child/teenager might feel abandoned; so they might act out in class; they might become involved in gangs, alcohol or even drugs. Some might withdraw into themselves feeling that life is very unfair.

Look at it this way, for us as adults if we lose a loved one in death, some of us do feel abandoned, and are left asking now what? We as adults are supposed to be older and wiser, what about the child/teenager who does not have the knowledge or life experience as that of an adult?

6. Feelings of loss can manifest through physical illness such as headaches, stomach cramps —when there is no physical basis for the symptoms.

7. For a child/teenager losing a guardian means confusion rules the day. Over whelmed, this young one's world is upside down; emotions will be all over the map. If the family is religious then the child/teenager might become angry at God and question why did God not save their loved one?

How to tell a child about a death.
Each child/teenager is different. Each situation will be different in respect to telling a child/teenager about a passing.

If you are the person breaking the news be aware of the child's needs, be sensitive!!!

1. Speak the truth about the death

2. Be direct
3. Relay the message in a simple and easy to understand manner
4. Make sure the child knows that they can/will be involved in the funeral/memorial service *IF* they choose. Let them know yes, they do *have a choice.*
5. Let the child/teenager know that their feelings are important.

Sudden Death

Sudden Death

I was reminded the other day, how things can happen unexpectedly. For example, those killed in the line of duty; police officers; our brave military men and women. Seldom do their families have warning.

Years ago, a neighbour across the way whose husband is in the military told me that she was terrified of receiving a late night knock at the door telling her, that her husband has been killed in the line of duty.

No notice or warning!!! The old saying "*To be forewarned, is to be forearmed*" comes to mind. Death is the most difficult thing to get ones brain around, even at the best of times; never mind when it is sudden.

Sudden death can be the result of just about anything; an accident, illness, crime or war. Many cases of very healthy people suffering massive heart attacks or a stroke it comes completely out of the blue. The news being delivered of a sudden death is very difficult to understand; never mind trying to make sense out of it. Really it does not make a bit of difference what has caused the sudden passing of a loved one. The hardest thing is accepting that they are gone forever. In your mind you know it; but in your heart reality has not sunk in.

The shock, trauma and pain almost paralyzes you, but not for long. There are plans to be made; decisions to be finalized; people to call. Now you feel as if you have just jumped out of a fast moving 747 *without* a parachute.

As adrenalin kicks in, you muster up the courage to do what is necessary to make funeral arrangements; choosing a plot; who is going to do the service? Here is one that I found extremely difficult, choosing an outfit for your loved one to be buried in. Sometimes you feel as if you are in some kind of a horrific nightmare and you will wake up and find out it was just a dream. Unfortunately, in this case it's a nightmare during the day and you are wide awake. So you somehow manage to make it through the funeral and now reality is starting to sink in.

No time to say good-bye; no time for last minute hugs and kisses. All long term plans that you shared and many dreams; are gone.

The biggest challenge comes when in cases of sudden death; if the deceased was pro-active, hopefully, there is a *Will* with a named executor in place. You will find on top of your grief there is now a mountain of paperwork than needs to be done.

Here are a few tips for you:

In spite of the cost, turn the will and all pertinent documents over to a reputable lawyer. Let them do the work for you. Trust me; you will not be in any shape to make decisions that could be life changing.

At this point you actually forget how to do the simplest of things. So making any huge financial decisions needs to be left to a later time when you can think with a clear head. There will be a few legal issues that need immediate attention, so just get the lawyer to address them.

After my husband's passing, it was recommended I sell our home and move. Thank goodness for a friend of mine who is a financial advisor. She basically told me NOT to make any major decisions for at least a year. From her experience; clients in similar circumstances, who made huge decisions to sell their home have told her that they made the biggest mistake of their lives. Unfortunately, you cannot turn back the clock, so to speak. Take time to heal. Join a support group. Talk to others that have survived loss. Speak to your spiritual advisor. Allow well- meaning friends to help you, even pamper you. This is not a betrayal of your loved one! If they were alive what would they advise you to do under the circumstances? More than likely they will say something to the effect of *'Life goes on, take the help, allow your friends to pamper you"*

Following Wayne's passing, having a few friends in really helped. Allow them to bring goodies such as wine, cheese, crackers and fruit; even goodies that your loved one enjoyed having. Celebrate your loved one; reminisce about times that you all shared together. Celebrate their LIFE! And you know what, if the *tears come that's fine too.* Keep the Kleenex box handy.

Death is difficult; whether expected, or sudden. Unfortunately life happens. All of us, including plant and animal life are here on this planet for a reason; as well as a season. We all will die at some point. This is reality.

Learning to cope with grief which I believe is the most difficult part of a human's life is essential for each and every one of us.

Suicide

Grief over the suicide of a loved one has it own emotional and psychological issues. There is this huge stigma around a suicide….. *what are the neighbours going to say when they find out?* Shame produces feelings of guilt creating personal emotions of being *judge and jury.* Due to these feelings of shame, families will make up a story to give to friends and other family members as to why their loved one has passed. Some family members are of the belief that if they had known perhaps there is something that they could have done to save their loved one. Perhaps there is also the nagging feeling that you might have said or done something to the individual that contributed to his taking his own life.

Think about this, when you make a decision to do something and you are *determined* to do it, can anyone talk you out of it? Let's say for a moment, someone convinces you to place your plan on the back burner. If you are hell bent on achieving your goal, chances are you will revisit it; until finally accomplishing what you set out to do? Someone deciding to end their life is no different. If they are determined; not asking for any help, they will, unfortunately, follow through with their plan.

I recently heard of a young woman (treated for cancer) who tried to take her own life. Although in remission, she could not afford the mounting medical bills after losing her job. Her family had been trying to help her out financially, but she was overwhelmed with guilt being dependant on others. The alternative in her mind was suicide. Now, in her case; she was found in time and is receiving the help and support that is vital for her.

Desperate people do desperate things

Survivors of a suicide can at times feel alone and alienated from everyone. In some cases a survivor might feel responsible that they did not do more to help a person that was depressed or someone that had lost their job. You feel perhaps it might have stopped the person from trying to take their own life.

Sometimes as a survivor, you too can feel lost and alone to the point of it becoming debilitating. These feelings within themselves can at times overtake you; at this point reaching your hand out to others for help is absolutely essential. Whether seeing your spiritual leader or a counsellor, seeking help is very important. This course of action will help you to realize that you are not responsible for someone else's taking their own life. *Forgive* yourself and your loved one!!

When a loved one commits suicide the family unit is torn apart. In many instances the family becomes angry; the feelings of betrayal and abandonment can mirror being punched in the stomach. Following a suicide; to heal you must work through the guilt and the anger.

Take the time to grieve and feel sorry. Make an effort to spend time with your friends. Recognize that within the suicide of your loved one there could be valuable lessons for you to learn.

Some might ask, "*What lessons could this possibly teach me?*" First of all, recognize all problems, no matter how huge, offer alternatives or solutions.

Second, a problem arises whether it is large or small, speak to someone about it do not keep it bottled up inside. Join a ***survivor group for peer support***. If such a group is not available join a ***bereavement support group***. The idea is; all have lost someone in death; no matter the circumstances, *grief is grief.* Support is very necessary for everyone involved.

NOTES

NOTES

Loss – Grief – Healing

Loss comes to everyone of us, and it can come in various forms.

1. Loss of a loved one -----**Bereavement**
2. Loss of a Job --------**Support for Self and Family**
3. Loss through divorce ---- **Loss of Companionship**
4. Loss of Self -------**No Sense of Direction; No Sense of Purpose**

However, in whatever way loss hits us personally, the point is we must work through this process. We as a society live in a death denying, grief dismissing world; we have no concept of how to handle loss. Society places enormous pressure on us to get over the loss, to get on with life and living.

We can truthfully say, in a moment of time, loss happens; lasting a life time.

Whether it is a loved one or a job, we go through grief. Grief is real because the loss is real. The pain of loss is very intense, it is heartbreaking. Grief signifies the loss of the connections that we came to rely on; to depend on. In many cases these connections nurtured us and made us the person that we have become. And now to have that connection severed is like having a piece of us ripped out. We are shattered; we are torn and rightfully so.

Grieving is the healing process that brings us comfort to deal with the pain of loss.

Healing grief is overwhelming and lonely, and in many cases we feel that we are not equipped mentally, physically or spiritually to handle the loss and furthermore our friends do not have a clue what to say to help us.

At times of loss, we find ourselves becoming fearful of life, our futures; we even fear making decisions. In time this fear gives way *to anger, isolation, sadness and self doubt.*

If we seek medical attention as a way to handle our loss, chances are we are given a prescription for either depression or to help induce sleep. Granted, there are occasions when these drugs are necessary. Yet in reality, we need someone to listen to us and give a few words of advice. Chances are a prescription is all that the medical profession can offer us. In reality what does a young doctor with no practical life experience have to offer someone going through loss? Some might read this and say, "*These doctors studied these scenarios in school*". Yes they did in theory.

I will say, I was very fortunate to have my family physician; who always takes the time to *first* of all listen to my fears and concerns and then to give some of his sage advice. He was extremely instrumental in the first few days following Wayne's death, to just sit me down and listen and of course see me cry; all the while keeping the Kleenex box within arms reach.

Society today is about the bottom line; money. In the case of an employee going through family issues, most companies are not tolerant in their attitude towards the employee. Their attitude is "If you cannot function in your job, we will find someone else". Little do they realize that it costs more to higher a new person that it is to support and help the present employee to regain their balance and once again become the productive individual that they have always been.

As a society we are challenged to find closure and find it quickly. Every one of us handles loss differently; some take longer than others. But even in the face of great loss, survival will happen; healing will take place. Do not forget the old adage that "*Time heals all wounds*".

When we lose someone particularly in death, we sometimes feel as if life has lost its meaning. The great lesson that I am learning is that "life is short". What we have lost in life will make us stronger and richer for having gone through the experience. You have *evolved*!

Time does heal, continue to give yourself permission to heal. By doing this you will once again be able to continue to *live* and *evolve*.

NOTES

Grieving To Heal

Some reading "*Grieving to Heal*" would respond with, *"Are you crazy", Grieving does not heal!! If this was the case how come I do not feel better, it's been five years since I lost my mother?*

My response to this question is, *"When your loved one passed, did you give yourself permission not only to mourn but also to grieve? Or did you suppress your emotions, allowing work or play to encompass all of your time and emotions?"* It's amazing the answers I receive. Everything from needing to get back to work, or not being able to take the time from work, other members need the support and so forth.

Major issues occur when we do not allow ourselves the opportunity to grieve. Grief affects our *spiritual, emotional and psychological* self. By suppressing our emotions we do not give ourselves the opportunity to heal our *soul, heart and psyche.* The grief process gives us the power to heal.

As a society we prolong our pain when we lose a loved one and do not go through the grief process. Grieving loss, if we give ourselves permission to grieve helps us to return to wholeness. Grief is uncomfortable; not only for us, but for people around us.

Six months after my husband's death —a well meaning friend said, "It's been six months; get over it." My response; though learning to live with the loss of Wayne; I will not get over it per se. Having spent the time going through the grief process is bringing healing to my soul and spirit. Grieving brings completion of a connection that will never be forgotten.

Perhaps some of you are in the early stages of grief. Your emotions are all over the map. At times you want to tear your hair out; at other times curling up under the covers brings comfort. Whatever helps you grieve needs to be done in order to heal.

Personally, I recommend finding an organization that will help you with the grief process. Also, seek out a good reputable Therapeutic Touch massage therapist; to calm the body, mind and spirit. Take frequent walks in nature. Slowly start to associate with friends, recognize that friends want to help but many times are clueless as to how to help. If there are things you need help with, ask for the assistance.

Become *introspective*. Again I repeat, start a journal. Take your fears; concerns and thoughts as a whole and commit them to paper. Journaling is very therapeutic. Meditate if possible.

It's been almost four years since Wayne's passing. My life has transformed. I am learning to live with the loss. There are many treasured memories. Continuing to love the man he was; I am continuously reminded about the many things he taught me. In growing and transforming, I am reaching out; to help others facing loss- this helps to show them that healing can and does take place after a loss. It takes time!

NOTES

Peace And Forgiveness

Peace And Forgiveness Begins With Us, An Introspective On Looking To Seek Wholeness Once Again.

The Ancient Hawaiian Healing Art of Ho'opnopono encourages us to take a real good look at every facet of our lives. For example *how* we deal with our internal conflicts this could be our fears, our doubts or even how we deal with family or even perfect strangers. This is critical if we are dealing with an end of life issue.

If there is a rift between family members, particularly if it is with the critically ill person, it is time to make peace! Making peace starts with you!!

In many cases years have gone by, and people cannot remember what caused the rift in the first place.

Ho'oponopono means taking one hundred percent responsibility for our lives; it means taking a real good look within our sub-conscious mind where many of our fears, doubts and judgments come from. The sub-conscious mind holds many of the emotional blockages that hold sway over us (The Self) today.

The sub-conscious mind is like a child that needs to be nurtured and loved. This nurturing comes from the ever- *conscious, present* mind. We must develop a rapport with it, do not ever think that the sub-conscious minds can be beaten into submission. Sorry this is not possible!! By quietly handling the subconscious mind, then the cleansing of all the negative *emotions, complexes* and *false identifications* can now begin. When these issues are converted into positives, we are now back in re-alignment within The Self as well as being in a place of clarity and inspiration. In turn these can lead us back to our soul's purpose. So, let's get started with how this cleansing can take place.

The words to the Ho'oponopono song begin with *"I am sorry, please forgive me, I thank you, I love you."* These words are very powerful within themselves and as humans we do not use them often enough. We must learn to use these words on a regular basis.

In order to forgive ourselves we must first take **COMPLETE** responsibility for *whatever happened or will happen in our life. So, we express the "I am sorry, please forgive me for whatever is happening within us (The Self) to have caused the situation to begin with.* By admitting and taking complete responsibility, we are also asking the Divine/Universe to expel blockages within our sub-conscious mind.

For example if we are in a relationship that is not serving our highest good our conscious mind recognizes the issues within the relationship. After much discussion between the two parties there is no resolution in some cases, the next course may be separation. However, the sub-conscious mind starts to lay the guilt about the misfortunes of a separation such as, *"Why upset the status quo? It is not that bad. Look at the amount of work it will take to split everything. What will your friends and family say about that this.......................... and the list goes on?"* When we look at our sub-conscious we will find that most of our guilt, fears, judgments etc have come from not just years but perhaps generations of old conditionings.

> *Dr. Wayne Dyer is quoted as saying…. "If you are living out of a sense of obligation – you are a slave"*

Peace and Harmony begins with each and every one of us as a person, we cannot live our lives for someone else. When we are not in harmony or in the flow, take a look within your self to see why you (The Self) are not at peace-----why you are not in harmony.

We (The Self) cannot look on the outside of who we are for the answers to our problems. We must look within.

Many of us seem to think that we are here to change the world. But really we cannot change the world. What we can do is to bring peace to ourselves as well as bring peace and harmony to the people that we interact with on a daily basis.

*"If you change the way you look at things,
the things you look at change"*
Dr. Wayne Dyer

We must remember that all things were created in perfect and divine order and that includes us as human beings. We are divine beings having an earthly experience. The issue comes in as to whether we perceive things correctly or not, guess what, most of the times we perceive them incorrectly.

At times, we meet people and we do not experience them the way we should---the way they were created. At this point we need to practice the Ho'oponopono cleansing by saying, *"I am sorry for whatever is taking place within me that I do not experience people in the image of how they were created. Please forgive me"*. By saying these words, we are slowly starting to cancel out old programming that is within our sub-conscious mind. We once again have clarity; we can now take a look at the person; recognize them for who they really are---A divine being, a person having a piece of the divine within them.

Let me clarify.

Envision this…………………..

Our brain is like a supercomputer with a very complexed memory system. It stores a vast array of information. However, at times some of the programs need to be deleted/erased/cleansed (Ho'oponopono) for various reasons. It could be the programs simply need to be updated or the programme has developed a virus which has now spread and corrupted all the programs within the memory banks of the computer. So the programs have to be deleted and new programming put into place, in order for the system to work at optimum efficiency.

So, Ho'oponopono means cleansing our heart, mind and spirit of things that is not serving us. A lot of this old programming comes from the sub-conscious mind.

Many people today, like to play the blame game; they blame everyone else for their problems in life; believe it or not there are people who even blame in this case their parents for having them come into this world. Little do they realize that they themselves choose not only their parents, but also the lessons that they want to learn in this lifetime. They will not/do not take 100% responsibility for their thoughts and actions. It is always someone else's fault. Again years and sometimes generations of programming has to be deleted from the sub-conscious mind. (The importance of doing the Ho'oponopono Cleansing)

This now leads to the next question: *"Once all of this stuff has been deleted out of the memory banks, then "Who am I".*

The answer is simply, ***We are Divine Beings having an Earthly Experience.***

Key component is: Divine Being. So ultimately we must take full responsibility for the things in our life and do not play the blame game. If we want to blame, then blame oneself, take 100% responsibility. As we take that responsibility, things around us change.

Think about this, is it our conscious mind that gives us the capacity to make the decisions to judge someone or to have doubts or fears? No, it is not the conscious mind, however by looking into the sub-conscious we can see patterns emerging as far back as our grand-parents or even further back in the family history that was very judgmental of people, whether these people might be of another country, ethnic background etc. If you feel as if you are being held back by negative energies, you are being held back from moving forward in any facet of your life, then its time to take a very serious and tough look within The Self. By doing this one will find their own negative emotions are the cause of the problem. Always remember that you are made up of divine energy, which means, that you have a light within. When cleansing/releasing of that negative energy is complete, not only do you open yourself up to that divine energy, but you also participate in that evolution of your soul or simply put you can now be back on track to discover your soul's purpose. If you believe that you are a victim, then this is the energy that you draw into your life. But if you believe that you are a divine being and that you want to emanate that light and love from the divine---you will draw positive things into your life. You will be a victor not a victim.

In this game of life we project to the world, through the decisions, beliefs and choices that we ourselves make. Everything in our consciousness is a result of reflection of you and your belief system.

What we perceive is what we believe. Why not work on perceiving what is correct that keeps us moving forward.

Again, extend the olive branch of forgiveness to family members while they are still alive and you are both able to have a conversation. Do not wait until the person has passed; it's too late then. In many instances your guilt surfaces.

You start to beat yourself silly over not having done something before now, I have heard too many people say "*Well I should have*", *or I could have*". It is simply too late.

NOTES

The Path That Grief Takes Us Through

The death of a loved one irrevocably changes us forever!! We cannot run or hide from the harsh reality of grief. This path that grief takes us through is very necessary to help us to move forward in our life's path.

Trust me when I tell you that this is not an easy path in any way shape or form, but we need to move through the various stages.

First let us define the two major stages of losing a loved and its impact on the very essence of who we are as a person.

The Grieving Process

This encompasses our entire thought pattern; it turns our emotions inside out. Our feelings on the inside bubble up. This internal mishmash of feelings go anywhere from being angry at your loved one for leaving you. To coping with friends and relatives who is trying to be supportive. But guess what at this point you are probably dealing with organizing the details of the funeral and handling all the paper work involved. Or perhaps you are going to do the eulogy yourself, the way I did.

The adrenalin kicks in. In order to survive, you push aside your feelings of grief.

The Mourning Process

The funeral is now complete, family and friends return to their homes and everyday way of life, often leaving you alone to cope. A few friends may check in on you. These occasions over time, become sporadic. You may spend more time in bed, pulling the covers over head. Depression may set in, as you tell the world to go away. You forget to eat or care not, if you ever eat again.

Now the memories come flooding back. You might replay the events surrounding the passing; confronting memories both good and bad.

Remember, mourning is different for everyone. Losing a loved one will probably be the most difficult thing you will ever have to face. Please remember, in order to heal we must first grieve. Acknowledge the reality of the death. When we lose a loved one----first acknowledge that we no longer have their physical presence in our life. In mourning we must embrace the pain of our loss. Although avoidance is easy, the pain will catch up with you when least expected. But by facing our pain head on, we reconcile ourselves to the reality of the situation.

We live in a society negligent in giving us adequate time to embrace our pain. Most employers expect an employee, suffering a loss, is entitled to take a maximum three day absence (if you are fortunate enough for three days, I have heard of a few companies that gives its employees one day for bereavement). The employee is then expected to return tow work and "*get on with it*".

Well meaning friends, sometimes not knowing what to say to someone who is in mourning, become an invisible presence. (what I mean by this is, instead of trying to sympathize, take the bull by the horns, prepare a meal and bring it over. Do the laundry etc.) Things such as these can mean so much to a person grieving.

Now there are the people that you will hear say, "*Keep your chin up*", or worse "*Stay strong*". *Trust me the last thing you want to do is stay strong. Crying yourself to death is more realistic.*

On the other hand there are people who have lost loved ones and can carry on as if nothing ever happened. I have found from experience, these people have not given themselves the time to grieve or to mourn. Something will eventually trigger all of the feelings and emotions of loss. In one case, a woman had lost her husband and within a month of this had sold their home and moved. She had disposed of all of the reminders of her loss. Six months later, she suffered a nervous breakdown. She longed to have something around her that belonged to her husband. But it was too late.

In my practice, I always admonish my clients dealing with loss – DO NOT make any major life altering decisions within the first year of the passing of a loved one. They are in no condition to make a sound decision emotionally.

Memory Reflection

No one can take away the memories we have of our loved ones; noweven more precious to us. Sometimes we will have very vivid dreams of our loved ones now in spirit.

Living with *memories* opposed to a *physical being*, entails a very different kind of *relationship*. Well intentioned friends will suggest you put away the photos of your loved one. It is YOUR RIGHT to keep the photos out for viewing for as long as you wish.

Lastly, remember when you embrace the past you make the way open for a future for yourself, a brighter tomorrow.

Our Identity; Who We Are

For years you were known as someone's husband or wife. Now, theterm "widower" or "widow." defines you.

A "parent" is now a "bereaved parent."

Part of who we are is identified by our relationships.

I remember the day of my husband's funeral. Standing at the grave site, I asked a friend of mine, "What do I do now?" Obviously my friend did not have an answer. So, I now had to take on a whole new role---being completely responsible for myself!!

Scary thought!!!

Everything I did was a first for me, handling all the bills, dealing with estate issues, budgeting to name a few. Because of the closeness of my relationship with Wayne it was extremely difficult to gain focus. I remember the first time I went grocery shopping after his passing; I walked into the grocery store. People were shopping, doing every day things; life went on as if nothing happened.

At the top of my lungs I wanted to scream, "*Wait a minute*! *Are you not sad "My husband died a week ago.*" Instead I ran out the grocery store in tears, the grocery list forgotten.

When one must take on complete responsibility for one's self, you are terrified of making a wrong decision. This is natural. There were times when I was overcome with feelings of frustration, helplessness and inadequacy.

However, over time, a sense of confidence and self worth emerges; empowering you to continue to go forward.

Why?

A woman, whose husband had passed, was so angry at god. "*Why" Did God have to take him?*

When you lose a loved one we tend to question many of our core beliefs; religious beliefs, our very purpose in this life, and even the meaning of life.

When we lose a loved one many times we ourselves feel as if a portion of whom we are died with him or her. We feel empty. Loneliness and sadness become good friends.

Having no control over death renders us powerless. It is said that death is an enemy. This is very true.

However, we DO have control on HOW we walk grief's path.

Support From Others

Do not try to walk this path of grief alone.

Recognize that this is a process that you are embarking on that takes time. Be compassionate with yourself! Recognize that each person deals with a loss in their unique way.

Draw on the experiences of others, seek out professional counsellors. Recognize that *seeking/needing* help is NOT a sign of weakness. As a matter of fact, it shows a great deal of courage and strength. Seeking help is a very healthy step to take.

Someone once said, "*When we open ourselves up for love, we also open ourselves up to possible loss and subsequently pain.*" This is a true statement.

Recognize that with having been loved as we had, we now need to honour that love by working through the grief and mourning process.

By doing this we honour not only our loved one, but we honour ourselves.

Now let me ask you a question:

Obviously you are going through a loss if you are reading this book. If your loved one was here how would they advise you to deal with coping with their death?

Chances are, first of all, they might apologize for passing when they did and subsequently putting you through this roller coaster of emotions. They might even ask forgiveness for their passing.

Then they would ask you to *please*, seek the help so you can move on with your life.

NOTES

NOTES

Prayer For You

Now that I am gone
Can you make it on your own?
I see your anguish
I feel your fear
I hear you gently crying
I can feel the pain within your heart

My prayer for you is

You will find love
The kind of love that will lift
the sadness from your soul
And bring laughter to your spirit

My prayer for you is

You will remember my promise
You will remember that I will
always be with you
For life goes on even on this side

My love, my life will go on
In your heart
In your soul

Where ever you go
I will go
Where ever you stay
I too will stay

My prayer for you is
Love, Light and Happiness
Until we meet again, dear one

NOTES

The Way of the Ancients. My Personal Voyage To Begin Healing

The road we walk in life can be filled with perilous twists and turns, and this includes the loss of a loved one.

There are times that we stand back, look at the road ahead saying, "No way, I am walking this road But really and truly do we have a choice or better yet any control on our walk?

Some might argue, "*Yes, we do have a choice.*" But do we really? Can we turn around and go back, maybe, but if we do so, are we running from the lessons we should be learning? Let me illustrate:

Wayne and I had planned on taking a trip to Hawaii at some point in our lives; before he passed he told me that I had to make the trip.

A few months after his passing, my depression and state of mind was so bad, in a dream I was told to get out of the house; do something, take a trip. If something was not done, I will literally die. Personally at this point in life; to me death would be a welcomed relief after losing my best friend, my husband.

It took some major convincing. Through a series of events, in a phone conversation with an acquaintance living State-side, I mentioned a possible trip to Hawaii. She asked me, "Where in Hawaii?" My response of, "Oahu" was met with dead silence, until she exclaimed, "Oh my god Ann, do you know where I live?" My memory somewhat vague, I responded, "Somewhere in the United States?" Can you imagine my surprise when she said, I live in Hawaii; downtown Waikiki."

We proceeded to discuss what I was looking for by way of a resort and it was simple, a place where it would be completely quiet, right on the beach, where I could listen to the sounds of the ocean.

With a bit of research it was decided on the Turtle Bay Resort on the North Shore of Oahu. So, credit card in hand my first solo trip was booked.

The flights in it self was uneventful, there was moments on the flight; I could feel Wayne and my Angels around me. There is a six hour time difference and the flight is twelve hours. Once I stepped off the plane, I came to the realization, in all the travelling that we had done over the years; this is one of the most beautiful islands in the Pacific. It was now a privilege for me to be visiting.

The Turtle Bay Resort that is located on the picturesque North Shore of Oahu was the perfect location for regrouping my life, thoughts and emotions.

As events transpired at check-in, my room was upgraded to an ocean front suite.

Jet lag, the time difference and being solo thousands of miles from home scared the dickens out of me. As the setting sun, in all its glory, reflected of the Pacific; stars twinkling in all their brilliance; I held my breath. What a sight to behold. From where I stood on the balcony, a knowing deep inside told me, it was right coming to this beautiful island! I knew my life was going to change in a profound way.

A flood of tears started; until sleep came at last, promising a beautiful tomorrow and the start of the renewal of soul and spirit.

The following morning, since my internal clock had not yet adjusted to the time change; saw me up at 5 a.m. PST. The sun was just starting to appear on the horizon. As I took a good look at the surroundings, I saw a formation of lava rock that extends out about half a mile into the ocean, and just a few feet wide. This lava formation has been in existence before anyone knew of the island's inhabitancy.

Being a person who likes to go where no man has gone before, on this gorgeous early Thursday morning, I decided to take a walk along the beach. Mind you, walking out on the reef was not part of any plan. Shining now in all its glory, the sun was inviting as it warmed my face. I walked, wiggling my toes in the warm, moist sand. A warm gentle breeze was blowing. It felt good to be alive despite my recent great loss.

As the walk continued, the reef came into view. I felt drawn to step on the reef. Flip flops now on my feet, I started my walk. A walk that would teach me many valuable lessons.

Listening to the sound of the ocean and the birds awakening to a new day, I felt the spray of salt water on my skin. This was a place of comfort, serenity and hope.

The reef started fairly smooth at first, led me to think this would be a cake walk. I was in for such a surprise!!!!! The reef became more and more treacherous; the lava being extremely sharp. I carefully chose my steps. Having presence of mind, I was in the here and now, known as *THE PRESENT*!!! As my steps slowed, I heard my inner voice speak to me, saying, "**You are walking The Path of the Ancients.**"

Stopping to look out at the beautiful blue and green ocean, I could hear and see the waves crashing against the reef, receding further back into the ocean, I could taste the salt (from the ocean air) on my skin and feel the gentle breeze whisper through my hair.

The ancients, knowing me to be a skeptic, at times repeated their message, "You are walking The Path of The Ancients." Okay, I get it!!! They proceed to ask me,

"Why do you always choose the roughest path to walk on? There are easier paths in which you can walk to reach your destination."

My tendency in life seems to be, taking the roughest road. Today was no exception to this rule. Standing atop one of the reef's highest peaks I really looked; at where my next step should be, with flip flops on my feet and the rocks as sharp as a razor, the next thought was, if I fall then what?

Suddenly I am having a momentary panic attack. In life, we all experience this at some time or another. Remember my earlier comment about that little inner voice?

Reminding me of my inherent ability to always make things more difficult for myself than necessary, the inner voice continues to say, "Ann, sometimes in life you need to stretch out you hand for help."

So, slowly I proceed on this walk, it becomes more difficult to place my feet on something fairly flat. At one point I started to move one foot ahead of the other, becoming instinctively aware that I could fall. So keeping in mind the "here and now; the present" and strictly concentrating on which steps to take, the walk continued.

Once again, the inner voice said to me, "Ann sometimes in life you need to stretch out you hand for help to reach your goal; now is a good time." The independent; stubborn person that I am, continued.

I observed huge crevices where the ocean eroded away some of the reef underneath, allowing waves to rush in. I did manage to cut the back of my heel.

Now, let me stop for a moment. I cannot answer for anyone else, but as an independent person; the premise is, I can make it on my own. However, I will admit; with the cut on my heel, instinct was to make my way back.

The little inner voice tells me, "No Ann, you have to trust us to help you make it through to the tip of the reef. So, I proceeded to move forward.

At times bending down very slowly and reaching out for help; holding on to a piece of lava in order to step forward. Trust now was a huge factor!!! My determination to reach the front end of this reef was greater than turning around and going back.

Carefully choosing my steps, I moved forward. From where I stood, the ocean extended for miles and miles. The turquoise, blue green color of the water was breath taking; looking down you can see schools of fish swimming by.

In the midst of everything, determined to capture the scene before me, I successfully took a couple of pictures. Quite nicely I might add!!!!

Guess what, sometimes in life we have to take a helping hand.

Amid the storms in our daily life, there can be some pleasant distractions that will invigorate us; to move us closer to our goals.

Onward and forward; as it became increasingly difficult to step forward; I was standing at the edge of the reef looking out at the waves lashing against the rocks. The sun seems to shine bigger and brighter than I had ever seen.

You see, I made it to the front of the reef, with a lot of help. As I turned to observe the path that I had taken in order to reach this point, it became very evident that this was not the easiest path to take. However the goal was accomplished! Yes, there was an easier way. Sometimes in life, we have to have determination to get to the place where we want to be the most.

We have to trust that inner voice to navigate the way for us, and at times we need to either lend a helping hand to someone or to accept a helping hand. The circumstances in which you find yourself will determine the necessary actions.

Walking The Path of the Ancients, made me realize that there are times we can make life a whole lot easier for ourselves. Ask for help. Listen to the instructions. Then trust and act on those instructions.

I now asked, The Ancients to show me an easier way back to firm ground. They did. The walk back to the sandy beach was easy, but cautious. I took a different route, yes; the lava was still sharp; there were twists and turns on this new route. But it was smoother.

Reaching back, from my point of departure earlier in the morning, I took off my flip flops; walked along the beach; sat down and looked back to where I had just come from.

I was thankful for the timely reminders. We must trust that inner voice to navigate the way for us. We must have the determination and courage to move forward.

Life can throw challenges in our path; such as the death of a loved one. How we circumnavigate the challenges will determine whether we will walk through an extremely rough lava field called life; determined to make it to the end, or will we walk through the same reef of life, but take the easier path, by listening and trusting the guidance of our inner voice. That inner voice is our Divine family; our angels; our guides and our loved ones trying to help us through the storms of life.

As for me, as stated earlier, it was not the plan to walk out onto the reef that beautiful Thursday. In retrospect, I am pleased that I did.

There were lessons that the ancients wanted to drum into my head. What better place for those reminders to be given, than on this beautiful island; walking along that reef where my inner voice told me, "You are walking The Path of the Ancients."

It's not necessary for a person to travel to Hawaii to heal; putting the pieces of one's life back together again.

Taking those first steps towards healing, by going through the stages of grief. Reach out, ask for the help you need, as you need it.

Recognize that you have friends wanting to help, who may not have a clue how to accomplish this. In some cases, they may feel it may be an intrusion.

Let them know it's okay to intrude.

In the meantime, *Mahalo Nui Loa* (Thank you very much) to the Ancients for continuing to guide and teach us; even though at times we do not recognize that this training is taking place.

Life has been changed in some very dramatic ways for me. Spirit has guided me to start an organization called Serenity of Hope. This organization works with folks going through end of life issues. With the help of my Angels, Guides and Wayne; I work to help people that have a fear of death to cross over with greater Clarity, Hope and Serenity.

The writing of this book is divinely guided to help many people cope with end of life issues and to remember that; "**We Are Never Alone.**"

Already in the early stages is a book called "Serenity's Poems to Healing and Wholeness." Another act of healing for me.

Life

As I sit and observe
The moon and stars

I reflect on my past
The good times
The bad times

The friends I have lost
The ones I have gained

I have started to write
And to live
A new story
A new life

What will this bring
I do not yet know

My wish and prayer is for
A new, healthy, wholesome
Loving relationship

For life is not the same as
I try to live it alone

Life and Love
Is meant to be shared

REFERENCES

Dr. Wayne Dyer ----- Inspirational Quotes

The Understanding Your Grief
By Alan D. Wolfelt Ph.D

On Death and Dying
Elisabeth Kubler-Ross, MD

Information also available through
The local Hospice Organizations

Dr. Ihaleakala Hew Len
Teacher of the Healing System of Ho'oponopono

ABOUT THE AUTHOR

Dr. Ann M. Ragobar is a Non-Denominational Minister, Lecturer, Grief Counselor and a Final Phase Transitional Facilitator. She is also Director of Serenity of Hope in Bolton, Ontario, Canada.